The Snow Prince
Copyright © 2024 by Lew Arrington

All rights reserved. No part of this publication may be reproduced, distributed, or transmitted in any form or by any means, including photocopying, recording, or other electronic or mechanical methods, without the prior written permission of the author, except in the case of brief quotations embodied in critical reviews and certain other non-commercial uses permitted by copyright law.

ISBN
979-8-3303-9575-0 (Paperback)
979-8-3303-9576-7 (eBook)

Dedication
Thanks to Amber and Virginia Arrington.

TABLE OF CONTENTS

Chapter One..1

Chapter Two...12

Chapter Three 20

Chapter Four 30

Chapter Five...40

Chapter Six 53

CHAPTER ONE

Once a long time ago in a land filled with beauty there was a kingdom. In this land there lived a people who were happy and were ruled by a noble Prince. This young man though young in years was humble and cared deeply for his people. Under his rule the land prospered. For he had been taught from an early age to respect those he governed. As a result, this land flourish and the kingdom prospered.

However, as happy as his people were under the rule of their prince. It was necessary for this young man to issue orders. When he did so, it was always to make his people safe from the dangers he knew would come. The rules were simple and made clear to those who lived in this valley. Knowing their ruler as a kind and caring young man. Those who lived in the villages willingly accepted the guidelines he issued. For they all knew with the coming of the Winter season. Harsh conditions would dominate their country with ice, snow and blowing winds.

Only these hardships were not the only known problems the people would face. Because along with the seasonal storms to come. They must also face another danger. This one would come down from the surrounding mountains. A threat to stir a deep sense of dread in the hearts of the people. Causing them to huddle in their homes for safety.

For along with the onset of Winter with its blowing snow and icy winds. A far greater danger was to come. Beasts forced down from their natural hunting grounds. Looking for fresh prey to fill their empty bellies. These animals were well known to those who lived in the villages in the valley. With the coming of Winter, these four-legged creatures would come hunting. Bringing their burning hunger with them when the snows covered the valley below. The villagers knew to expect this danger. And with the coming of the first heavy snowfall. Those who lived in the valley must be prepared for the coming of the Mountain Ice Wolves!

As the days passed the people worked hard to collect the crops from the fields and groves. Their young prince out among his people encouraging them to collect the food they would need to survive. Making haste to gather and store the supplies needed for the long Winter. With the guidance and encouragement of their gentle ruler. Each day brought the harvest closer to being completed.

As the Winter season approached this tiny kingdom, the prince devoted himself to his tasks. Among these were not only collecting the food needed for his people. There were other concerns he must plan for. Such as the coming danger of the Mountain Ice Wolves. These were serious concerns for the young royal. However, another pressing issue he faced was equally daunting. For there was the threat coming from roaming bands of bandits. Men intent on plundering his kingdom and harming his people. It was his duty to guard against these raiders. Which was why he would spend hours with his royal guards. Seeing to it they were prepared to face any armed intruder.

This was a responsibility the prince was determined to carry out. Keeping the homes and property of his people safe from evil men. For the prince had heard many stories of looters attacking other kingdoms. This was a troubling concern the prince kept uppermost in his mind. Aware of this burden to his people. The prince sent out soldiers to patrol the valley. Always watchful for the coming of strangers.

So his days were filled with the requirements brought on by his royal station. Not only to prepare for Winter by gathering the crops needed to feed his people. But to heed his concerns when it came to the safety of the kingdom. As a result, there was little time for rest. From first light until long after sundown the prince would toil. Knowing all too well the Winter storms were coming. But thanks to his commitment. The supplies were filling the storehouses in the villages. This accomplishment, caused the prince to breathe a sigh of relief. Even so, there was no time for the young royal to rest.

Each day found him either out with the field workers. Or seeing to the training of his soldiers. Doing his best to supply the encouragement each group needed. He was always aware they were doing their best to serve him. Then each evening the youth would spend hours at his desk. Attending to reports concerning all manner of the issues of his kingdom. But there was always the pressure of time lingering in the back of his mind. Winter was drawing closer with every day that passed. Bringing the looming threat of the Mountain Ice Wolves.

But even a prince must rest. Trudging his way to his own chambers. The youth would carry his lamp in hand through the silent halls of his castle. Only to lay awake on his bed as his burdens remained in his thoughts. Until at last sleep claimed him. But dreams of the terror to come rose to haunt his slumber. Until the first rays of dawn caused him to wake. Each day bringing more tasks to fill his day. Duties only he could perform.

After a quick breakfast, the young man set out to the stables. There he saddled his horse then rode to the gate. On this day, the prince paused to issue a set of instructions to one of his soldiers. Messengers must be sent out to warn the villagers of the coming danger from the mountains. The Ice Wolves would arrive with the first heavy snowfall. When the ground was covered and the drifts were deep. Each of his subjects must be safely indoors before sunset.

Because during the long nights, the ravenous beasts were known to roam through the streets. Any citizen who found themselves outside after nightfall. Risked an attack by the roving and dangerous packs. The people were only safe during daylight hours. At dawn, the beasts always slunk back to the dense forests. Allowing the people to venture out to conduct their daily business. With his orders given, the prince headed for the nearby fields.

Making haste, he rode to where his people were hard at work in the groves and fields. Looking out over the activity of his people, the prince found himself nodding. This year's harvest had gone well. Feeling a smile come to his face, the prince felt a sense of relief. The wagons were almost fully loaded. Once they were, it was only a short journey to the storehouses.

It was not long before the heavy wagons lurched toward the waiting village. Then the prince turned his gaze toward the nearby forest. This was where the Ice Wolves would soon be lurking. Sitting in his saddle, the young royal found himself pausing in thought. After a few moments he came to a decision. It was time for him to call in his experienced hunters. They were the best individuals to watch for the first signs of the deadly beasts. However, the young man must consider the risks the trackers must face.

For this reason, he made a command decision for their safety. When they did venture out looking for signs of the packs from the mountains. They were to go in larger groups and not as single hunters. In this way, they all stood a better chance against the dangerous animals. At the same time, the prince came to another decision. It was time for him to increase the number of soldiers patrolling the borders of the forests! Keeping the wild hogs living in the woodlands away from the fields was important. This was not a dangerous task. This was not a dangerous task. But it kept the little beasts from ravaging the fields.

In his mind, the prince felt increasing the number of soldiers on patrol served a dual purpose. First, with the guards moving along the edge of the forest. The activity would serve to keep the wild hogs confined to the undergrowth of the woodlands. The idea the prince had, was to prevent the hogs from escaping to damage the fields. Second, and even more important to the prince. Was the need to reduce the growing hog population. If his plan worked, the Ice Wolves would stay in the deep woods until the end of Winter.

This plan, might also keep the people in his kingdom safer. The activity of his guards should prevent the hogs from escaping the woods. In this way, when the Ice Wolves came down from the mountains. Hopefully, they would reduce the hog population during the long Winter. So that when Spring finally returned. The wolves would leave the valley with fewer hogs. Thus the threat to the freshly planted crops might be reduced. By them moving along the edge of the forests. The soldiers kept the wild hogs confined to the undergrowth. In the mind of the prince. He hoped this action would prevent the wolves from venturing into the villages. Because if the dangerous predators were hunting hogs. His people would be safer with the wolves away from the villages. While at the same time, it reduced the numbers of these smaller beasts. Who were a constant pest when it came to the farmers growing crops.

CHAPTER TWO

As the prince continued to stare at the nearby forest. He was forced to accept a hard truth. When Winter did arrive, his people would have to remain indoors after nightfall. But at least his actions served to protect the villagers. It was the best solution he could think of at this point. No matter he told himself. His subjects understood the reason for his precautions. In the past, it had kept them from harm. Even if they had to remain indoors after nightfall.

Turning his gaze away from the now empty fields. He looked toward the nearby village. It was at that moment; he saw the last of the loaded wagons turning a corner. With a nudge, his steed was in motion. It was his intention to be at the warehouse as the food supplies were moved into the storehouse. After all, this was just another part of his duty to his people. For his own piece of mind, he needed to see how full the buildings were. Arriving at the warehouse, the royal youth watched his people at work. Their efforts a clear sign they saw their tasks as important.

It was just after midday, when the last of the Winter food was at last stored. And the prince was preparing to return to the castle. Smiling, the youthful royal knew this year's harvest was a success. In his mind the young man knew the people would not go hungry this Winter. Leaving the warehouse, the prince mounted his horse. Looking past the nearby buildings. The young man found his gaze going to looming peaks of the not-too-distant mountains.

Feeling a gentle breeze caress his cheeks. The prince was reminded of a simple fact. The Winter storms were coming and very soon the valley would be covered in ice and snow. This daunting fact came to him while he was sitting on his gentle horse. His next thought brought on even more concern for him. There was only one way into or out of the valley.

In one way this was a blessing. With the coming of the snows, the way into the valley would be blocked!

When this happened, the threat of bandits would be less likely. As the marauders would be unwilling to enter on foot. Their horses unable to slog through the deep drifts of snow. Unfortunately, the prince also realized with the gap between the mountains blocked. No traders could bring in fresh supplies for the villagers. At least, not until Spring brought warmer weather to melt the ice and snow. This unpleasant revelation caused him to frown. Then with a shake of his head, the prince accepted the reality.

With the coming of the ice and snow. His people must wait for Spring to open the pass. It was in this moment when the young prince felt a deep feeling of isolation come over him. While his people had their families and friends to provide companionship. He knew he must spend the fridged and bone chilling Winter alone. Now more than ever, the young man missed his parents. The two people who had made life in the castle bearable. Shaking his head, the youth knew he must keep his focus on his people. They needed him to be strong for the coming Winter. His own happiness must be put aside, for now.

A few days later when the prince was out training his soldiers on an empty field. One of his guards who had been with a squad at the narrow pass came galloping up. Upon reaching the field, he searched for his prince. It did not take long for this warrior to find him. Riding up the man saluted his young ruler. The guard then delivered the news. A large group of travelers in a caravan were entering the valley.

With a note of concern showing on his youthful face. The prince ordered the captain of his royal guard to gather some of his soldiers. Having had experience with outlaws on other occasions. There was the possibility of bandits hiding within such a large group. What the prince needed, was for his soldiers to inspect this arriving caravan. His concern must be met with action to safeguard his people! Because if there were any bandits hiding in this band of travelers. It must be discovered before they reached the villages!

It was hours later when the captain of his guard came to find him. Locating his prince astride his horse out on one of the barren fields. The captain saw the young ruler watching his troopers as they trained. Easing up to his superior, the captain of the guard reported. The caravan had been fully inspected and no bandits had been found. The warrior also informed his prince of the wide variety of items these traders had come to barter.

Smiling, the prince understood instantly the importance of what this man had reported. This caravan was likely to be the last one to come into the valley before snow began to fall. His people would welcome these traders with great fanfare. Because there were items they would need before the coming of Winter. Having listened to his captain with a growing joy. The arrival of these travelers would add to the planned celebration of the just completed harvest. Knowing there was much to do. The prince turned to his loyal guard captain and issued some instructions.

Knowing what his prince intended, the loyal soldier set to work. There were actions he must now undertake. The royal guard must prepare for the coming of the new arrivals. Upon hearing the news of the traders, the soldiers were filled with real joy. Visitors did not arrive every day in the kingdom. Each of them knew there were tasks they must now undertake. A suitable campsite must be prepared for the coming of this traveling band of merchants. Just as important was the duty to spread the news to the villages. As the people would want to prepare items they would want to trade.

But first, there was the more important task of preparing for the Fall Festival. This event would now be even more festive for the people. Because soon, there would be fun, dancing and music bringing joy to everyone! So it was, the traders came rolling in with shouts of welcome. Then the merchants went to work at their new campsite. The men and women of this caravan needed to unload the items to be traded. In return, the peddlers would take what the villagers had to offer. Fresh fruit, vegetables, and other items the people had made.

In the nearby castle, the prince found himself smiling. In his mind, the unexpected arrival of the traders was a good omen. Not only would his people benefit from the trading to come. But the kingdom had been preparing for the annual Fall Festival. With the arrival of these traders. The celebration would be even more joyous! But after the music, dancing, and games. There would be active and spirited trading. While the prince could look forward to hearing of the world beyond his kingdom. Taking a moment, the royal youth went to the battlements of his castle. From this high vantage point, he looked out to where the traders were setting up their camp.

It was hours later when the prince was informed the traders had made camp. Calling his captain of the guard, the two men mounted their horses. Then leaving the castle they urged their steeds to gallop through the gate. With the wind whipping his long hair. The prince and his guard captain headed for the newly established campsite. Upon his arrival, he went searching for the leader of this band. In no time at all, he was speaking with this smiling and jolly man.

After issuing a warm welcome to the chief of these traders. The prince was introduced to other important individuals within the caravan. Being a courteous host, the prince then invited these heads of families to a lavish banquet in their honor. With a bow, each of those gathered individuals accepted the gracious offer. Turning their horses, the prince and his captain returned to the castle. For there were many actions to be taken. Orders to be given for the coming feast. Within a short time, the castle was filled with sounds of joyous activity.

Once all the careful preparations were complete. It was time for the Harvest Festival to begin. By late afternoon, the people began to come together. Both the merchants and the villagers were ready to celebrate. In no time at all, there was the sounds of laughter and music. While in the castle, the prince welcomed the leaders he had invited. Soon everyone was seated and the feast began. Long into the night, those in the castle enjoyed all manner of entertainment.

While out on the festival grounds, the villagers and traders ate, sang, and danced the night away. Late into the evening the sounds of laughter could be heard. Filling not only the campground, but the castle as well. Until it was time for bed. As the sun dipped below the surrounding mountains the attendees finally ended the festivities. With the light from burning torches to guide them. The traders went to their wagons. While the villagers returned to their homes.

Even so, he found himself considering what else he could do to safeguard the citizens who looked to him for safety. For not only would the Winter bring a bitter Season of cold. But the fearful threat of the beasts from the high mountains. For the Prince, it was his duty to protect those within his kingdom from these dangers.

It was later that day, when the escorting soldiers reported to their prince. The caravan had made it safely through the gap in the mountains. In the days to follow, the winds began to blow with a fearsome intensity. This was a reminder to the people of the valley. Winter would soon be upon them and they had final preparations to make. Until one day the wind brought with it a biting cold. Followed by the first heavy snowfall. This warning was understood by all. The Mountain Ice Wolves would soon arrive.

Short days later the force of the winds increased to a howling screech. Bringing with it more freezing ice and snow. Warm and safe in their homes the people were prepared to wait for Spring. For his part, the prince knew this season of cold would pass. When at last Spring returned with its warmer weather. The dangerous wolves would go back to their mountain home. As if to underscore this reality. A soldier arrived to inform him the gap to the valley was now blocked!

CHAPTER THREE

In the days that followed, more freezing storms came rolling into the valley. Leaving a heavy blanket of fresh snow across the valley floor. From time to time the prince would venture out onto the high ramparts of his castle. From this vantage point, he could see his kingdom choked with snow. Staring out over the landscape. He felt his cheeks being stung by the ice blown wind. Until at last he turned away. Forced to return to the warmth of his castle.

Upon entering his study, the young ruler sat before his warming fire. His mind going to the issue of the soon to arrive Ice Wolves. Very soon, these beasts would be stalking the land. Brought down from their normal hunting grounds due to lack of food. Shaking his head, the prince could only sit and wait for the coming of these beasts. A dangerous predator combining with the harsh and frigid conditions just beyond his castle walls. Aware he had done all he could for his subjects. He could only wait out the harsh and unforgiving Winter!

Even so, the prince felt compelled to consider what else he could do to safeguard the citizens of the valley. The heavy burden of responsibility always on his mind. Then the day arrived when a group of hunters reported to their prince. During their most resent search near the borders of the forests. They had found signs the dreaded beasts from the mountains had arrived. Having received this warning, the prince knew he must send out a warning to his people.

Calling for the captain of his royal guard. The prince now issued a new command. The people must be told the wolves had arrived. Once informed of this returning danger. His people would take more precautions to guard themselves. Because it was well known how silent and dangerous Mountain Ice Wolves could be! Upon receiving the command from the prince. Soldiers went out to every home in the valley. Everyone was to be indoors before dusk. This action would keep them safe during the long and bitter nights.

    This was not the only command the prince gave his loyal troops. With the coming of sunrise, squads of soldiers set out to check on his people. Making sure they had survived the long cold night in safety. Then the troopers would head for the borders of the forests. There these groups of men would remain on guard. Mounted and with their weapons at the ready. It was hoped the soldiers could keep the wolves confined to the forests. Because it was known these four-legged beasts seldom attacked mounted soldiers.

But as dusk approached, his loyal guards would return to the safety of the castle. Because at night, with a deep burning hunger. The Ice Wolves would come hunting for food to fill their ravenous bellies! Since the members of these roving packs were natural night hunters. They were able to slink into the villages under the cover of darkness. Intent on finding anyone unfortunate enough to be out after nightfall.

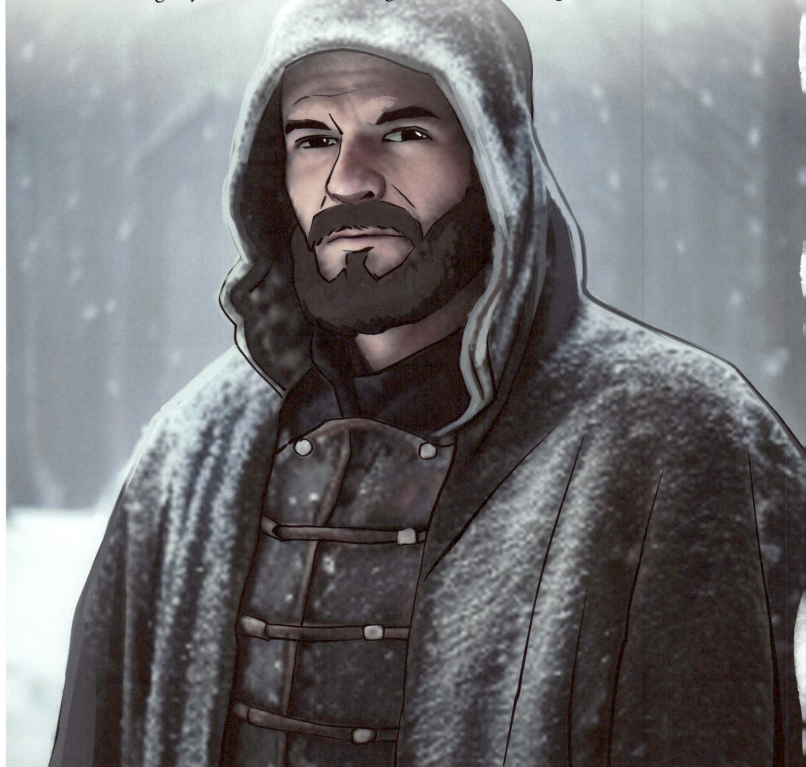

Having done all he could to safeguard his people. The prince could only wait out the harsh Winter. In the meantime, he continued to worry inside the ice-covered walls of his castle. Sitting in his study, he would have to wait for Winter to pass. With a warm fire burning before him, he took down a volume to help him pass the time. But there was no way for him to know what was happening beyond his walls.

Meanwhile, a lost stranger was battling for his life. His caravan had been attacked and he had become separated from his companions. Now he was struggling to make his way through deep drifts of snow. Desperate to find some measure of safety in the lashing and bitter snowstorm. For a fleeting moment this man found his thoughts going to the men who had traveled with him. But an instant later, he was pelted with ice and snow from a heavy gust from the blizzard. Cold and shivering, this man was forced to renew his efforts to find any form of shelter.

Now this man looked around at the white dunes of snow awaiting him. For a moment he felt a wave of despair. This was quickly followed by his determination to keep going. He might be lost and isolated in this barren land of ice and snow. However, he had no intention of giving up! Calling on his inner strength, he pressed on. Moving with difficulty through the dark land that surrounded him. After what felt like hours of struggle. The man felt his strength failing. It was clear to him he must find shelter and soon. Or risk freezing to death in this barren white landscape.

Determined to find a haven until this storm passed. The older man paused to look around him. Only to see a wall of blinding snow blocking his vision. While at his feet, mounds of drifting snow grew deeper. No matter he told himself, he would continue to search. For in his mind there must be a place where he would find sanctuary. Any place with a warm fire. Anywhere to wait out the Winter Storm now raging all around him.

As he stood with his feet deep in the snowdrifts. He could find no trace of a path for him to follow. For the blowing snow had covered the ground as far as he could see. And that was not very far. But as chance would have it, he stumbled into a wall of rock. Then he fell through a gap in the mountains. A pass that would lead him to a remote valley. This was a stroke of luck that would allow him a chance at survival.

Lurching along through the buildup of snow and ice. He soon found himself at the other end of the gap in the mountains. Instantly the wind increased and it threatened to engulf him. But this man was unwilling to give in to the wind and snow as it continued to block his way. Instead, he forced himself to drive himself ever forward. His will to live a burning force within him. But another challenge awaited him as he strove to move forward.

The long hours in the freezing cold was taking a toll on this man. As a result, every step required him to exert more energy just to move forward. Doing so was a drain on his fading strength. But being who he was. There was no choice left to him but to press on. To give in to despair was not in his nature. Even though the freezing cold clawed at him with fingers of ice. Striving to draw what remained of his warmth from his body.

Feeling he was close to collapse in this white blank landscape. This man was desperate to find any form of shelter. Pausing to look around, he felt a growing sense of despair. There was no doubt in his mind the storm was growing worse with every passing moment. Its continuing assault on him making it difficult to see. If he did not find help soon, he was doomed. Then reaching down to his inner core, the traveler summoned a grim resolve. If it took every ounce of his determination. He would not submit to this cold unrelenting Winter.

Pausing in the blowing ice and snow. The stranger took a moment to pull his arms around himself. Striving to keep his inner warmth from escaping. Then once again he set out and pushed forward. Attacking the next snow drift as if it were a mortal enemy. His only thought was to achieve the only thing that mattered at this point, victory! For he was convinced there was a haven waiting just past the next mound of snow. All he had to do was reach it before the cold overcame him. It was in this ice clutching moment when he heard it.

A sound far colder than the ice and snow all around him. The long wailing cry of an animal. This sound was quickly followed by the yelping of more calls. Sounds that were coming out of the blizzard. While the chilling storm around him sucked at his inner warmth. The sounds of the animals out in the darkness were enough to freeze his blood in fear. Even as he stood hoping he had been mistaken. The wailing cry came again only this time it sounded closer.

Seconds later, he was able to identify with growing fear the howling scream of a hunting pack. One that signaled the beasts had found the trail of its next victim. And in his mind there could be no doubt. The hunting pack had come across his tracks in the snow. As if to confirm this dreadful belief. There came another sharp yapping bark followed by a terrible howl. Instantly the lost man knew, the hunting pack was drawing closer!

From his past he found himself remembering the hunting call he had heard as a youth. Only this time he was the one being hunted. With the memory from long ago filling his brain. The lost stranger knew there was only one option open to him. He must run! Run to save his life from the fate that was coming for him now! With a sudden burst of fear inspired energy. The man lunged forward, creating a path through the drifting snow before him.

But his progress was slow and labored against the wind blowing against his body. With ice shards filling the air all around him. While behind him there came another keening call of the hunting pack. The sound of their combined voices drawing ever closer. With his resolve spurred on by the sounds coming out of the darkness. The stranger did his best to urge his half-frozen limbs to work harder. Needing to put distance between him and coming death.

For an instant, his brain latched onto a half-realized wish. Perhaps the shroud like darkness around him would hide him. But with the next yapping shriek of the pack. The lost stranger knew he had only one hope. He must find shelter and quickly. A barrier to keep the wolves with their fangs and claws from tearing him apart. With his heart pounding, he fought to put distance between himself and coming animals.

Fighting from snowdrift to snowdrift. The lone fugitive from death struggled with every step he took! However, the sound of the pack told the man the animals seeking him were closing the distance. No doubt aided by their keen sense of smell. Their howling cries a clear indication of how close they were. An ordinary man might have given up. Letting his body fall into the waiting snow for the beasts to find him. But this was not a common man who would ever give up. He would keep going until his very last breath was torn from his chest!

In a castle not far away, two soldiers stood guard in an alcove warmed by a glowing stove. These troopers were on duty at the front portal of the castle. It was full dark and the gates were closed and locked. Even so, these sentries knew they must continue to be vigilant. As they remained at their post within the enclosed fortress. They heard a sound to freeze their hearts in their chests! It was the hunting call of the dreaded Ice Wolves. A sound like the howling scream of the damned! Having lived in this kingdom all their lives. The two men quickly recognized the yelping call. It was a hunting pack on the trail of some unwary prey.

Looking at each other with a knowing expression. The two soldiers felt a wave of concern. There was no doubt what the baying meant. The only question they had, was what were the beasts hunting? Knowing their duty and the wishes of their prince. The guards moved to the portal that protected the castle. To open this gate would present a danger to these men. No matter, it was their duty to check for a possible lost villager? Someone who had been caught out after dark?

But there was a risk in taking this action. For it was known to every soldier in this kingdom. When opening the gate, danger might be right outside. Though the menace from roving bandits might have been reduced. It could not be discounted entirely. But more importantly, was the peril of the Ice Wolves getting into the castle grounds. No doubt they would perish at the hands of the royal guards. But the havoc they could bring was not to be ignored. For this reason, the soldiers must be on guard. But just as the guards reached the entrance to the castle grounds. Another howl came that was far closer than it had been before. In this moment the soldiers knew they must act!

CHAPTER FOUR

Beyond the ice coated castle walls a dangerous drama was now playing out. For out of the raging storm there came the stumbling shape of a man. Blinded by the blowing Winter winds and caked in ice and snow. The traveler could barely see what lay in front of him. His eyes all but blinded due to the blizzard. His coat, eyebrows and beard coated from the heavy snowstorm. Marking him little more than a walking snowman. As if children had created him from a newly fallen snowfall.

Driving forward the half-frozen man fell against a solid wall of stone! But as his breath was knocked from his cold wracked lungs. There came the frightening sound not far away. The hunting pack was dangerously close now. The Ice Wolves convinced their next meal was only moments away. Their long chase was coming to an end! It was in this moment that destiny tipped the balance in this drama. And in the process, spared the life of a half-frozen stranger.

Because suddenly from out of the swirling blizzard came heavy hands to rescue the stranger. The two sentries acted as they had been instructed. Grabbing this unknown and exhausted man, they dragged him through the portal. Once inside the fortress, one of the guards turned to lock the portal. All in an effort to keep the wolves from entering the castle grounds. Once he had it secure. He helped his fellow guard place the half-frozen man next to the warming stove.

It took several long minutes before the rescued stranger was able to gather his wits. Slowly he recognized he had been saved from the jaws of death. However, when he turned to thank his rescuers. He quickly discovered he was not truly safe. For he found himself facing two armed warriors with weapons drawn. In the next instant, he was jerked to his feet. Then he was quickly marched into the heart of a castle.

Still shivering from his bone chilling journey through the raging snowstorm. The stranger soon found himself facing a new concern. Though he had cheated death by escaping the still howling beasts outside the castle walls. He now found himself about to be judged in a room filled with unfriendly eyes. Some of them warriors with drawn swords. Looking around the large room, the stranger did not see a single smile on the faces of those gathered here.

Half frozen, with no weapons and there being so many soldiers surrounding him. The stranger knew there was no way he could have put up any resistance. Nor did he want to risk angering the young man seated in front of him. In his mind, he was hoping for a chance to explain how he had come to be here. However, he could feel the tension and growing suspicion of the people in this room. Looking at the person on the throne. It became obvious he was about to be judged.

Taking a quick glance around the room. The stranger came to a simple conclusion. This was no doubt the castle of someone of royal birth. The traveler could only assume this man was a prince. Which meant, he had stumbled into a remote kingdom. With an effort, he tried to recall where he had been when his caravan had been ambushed. If he were right. This must be the youth who now ruled after the death of his parents.

Looking around, the cold and shivering traveler found himself marveling at the size of this room. From his current position, he could only marvel at what he was seeing. But an instant later, he reminded himself he was not safe yet. No doubt he was about to be judged by this young prince. After all, he had arrived during a snowstorm. He was not a subject of this ruler. There was reason to view him as a threat to this young man's kingdom. If he wanted to go free. He must convince this young royal he was not a bandit.

Taking a closer look at the older man standing to one side of the prince. It was easy to judge the rank of this man. He must be the commander of the soldiers in this kingdom. But another searching glance cause the traveler to grow more concerned. The expression on the face of this older warrior did not show any signs of warmth nor welcome. In fact, the man was standing with his sword in his hand. As if he expected to use it in this very room. This was not a good sign.

On the plus side, this royal youth had a kind face. And appeared to be looking him over with great care. Perhaps there was a chance he would be judged fairly. There was no way to know until the prince spoke. But in the meantime, it was best he remain silent until someone spoke to him.

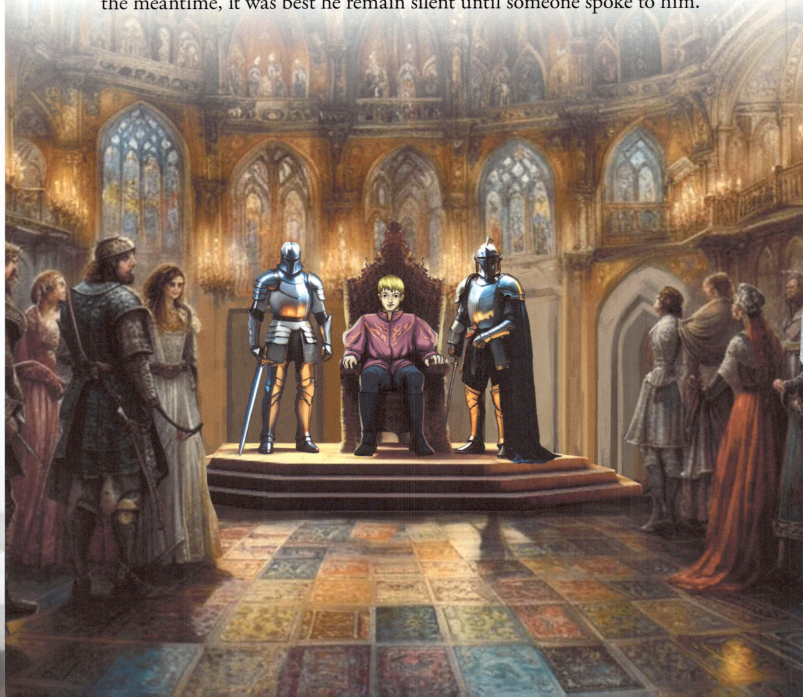

After a careful inspection, the prince realized the man in front of him was not one of his subjects. The clothing he wore did not come from any of the villages within the kingdom he ruled. It was very clear to the prince this man was a stranger. For this reason, he must be judged to determine if he was a danger to the people who looked to the prince for protection. Uppermost in his mind was the threat of bandits who in the past had harmed his people. Now he must judge and determine the fate of this stranger.

Upon questioning of the two gate guards. It was quickly revealed how this stranger had come to enter the fortress. The story the sentries told was simple enough to grasp. Having heard what his soldiers had to say. The prince turned to the silent stranger. Giving the individual another searching look. The prince found himself wondering what this man would tell him. Afterall, it was foolish for anyone to be out in such a storm. Not when the Ice Wolves were lurking in the dark.

Having been informed of the fact this stranger had been pursued by deadly beasts. There was no reason to doubt the story his soldiers had told him. For the young prince had every reason to trust their loyalty. As the soldiers in the great hall waited in silence. The prince found himself frowning as he pondered the decision he must make. He knew he could not risk the safety of his people. For there was no way he could be sure this stranger was not a bandit in disguise. The treachery of those bandits in the past was well known. However, casting someone out to face the Ice Wolves was not a decision to be made lightly. This meant, he had to discover the truth. How and why had this man come to his castle?

Standing silently before the prince. The stranger was caught in a daunting delima. To save himself he must tell this royal youth the truth. Only he must be cautious in an effort not to reveal too much. Because there was power in knowing who someone was. Even so, if he did not convince this prince of his innocence. He could very well be cast out into the waiting jaws of the wolves. And they would extract a fearful and final judgment upon him.

Seeing the expression on the young royal change. The man being questioned knew he must make a final plea. For there was no doubt in his mind. Once this youth issued his judgement. Nothing would change the decision and his fate would be sealed. For this reason, the stranger looked up and addressed this ruler.

"Noble born. I am a stranger who means no harm to you or your people. I was on my way home when my caravan was engulfed in a building storm. As we were making camp, a band of outlaws attacked us. During the battle I became separated from those who traveled with me. Due to the raging blizzard, I became lost in the snow. For that reason, I was unable to return to the safety of my comrades." The stranger explained. Trying to convey the truth of his words.

Looking upon this stranger the prince faced a daunting conflict of conscience. How was he to know the truth? To make a mistake in judgement could place his kingdom and its people in danger. However, to condemn this man out of fear did not feel right to the prince. There seemed to be only two choices for him to choose from. Freedom with the chance of betrayal. Or consign this man to the waiting Ice Wolves still lurking beyond the castle walls. It was a heavy decision where he must find balance and fairness.

Seeing the prince was close to a final judgement. The stranger made a split-second decision that would change his life forever. Clearing his throat the stranger spoke out in a clear and steady voice. While this prince and his people listened, the stranger spoke. Filling his voice with the conviction of his innocence. He turned his full attention to the prince who would soon judge him.

"My lord. If it should please you I only ask for sanctuary from a cold and bitter death. I can understand the delima you face. There might seem to be only two possible choices open to you when it comes to my fate. Cast me out to the fearful beasts who will surely devour me. Or to free me and thus risk your kingdom. I would suggest there is a third possibility. Lock me in one of your castle dungeons. In this way I will be spared being torn apart by the beasts outside. Then you can hold me until Spring. At which time I can continue my journey back to my own home."

At this point a hush filled the room. Everyone who had gathered here found themselves turning to their prince. It was now time for him to announce his ruling. Watching this young prince. The stranger did not know what his judge would decide. Then a sudden change in expression came to the face of this young ruler. All of those who waited knew a decision had been made.

Quick to sense a coming verdict the servants and soldiers eased forward. No matter what was decided by their prince. The guards would do their duty and carry out his orders. Even so, these hardened men did not relish casting this man out to the waiting wolves. In response they all shuddered at the thought of such a dreadful fate. Only this was not their decision to make. For them it was a simple matter of doing their duty to their prince!

Taking one last look at the stranger before him. The prince had noted several critical facts that had not gone unnoticed. The clothing might be torn and soiled but they revealed a man of wealth. Plus, the man spoke and acted as a man of honor. These facts told the prince this man was not a bandit. Nor was he a simple traveler. Obviously, there was far more to this stranger than what had been revealed.

In the end, the dignity and inner bearing of this man was the deciding factor for the prince. The royal youth found himself convinced not to cast this man out to face death. Instead, he turned to his gathered servants and made his final ruling known. With a firm command the ruler of this kingdom spoke.

"Free this man!" The prince said. Then began to issue detailed instructions to his staff. For their part, the guards and servants were quick to react to the commands of their youthful prince. Sheathing their swords, the soldiers stood back. While the servants moved forward to carry out their new instructions. Moments later they were showing the traveler to a guestroom.

Startled that he was not to be thrown to the howling wolves beyond the castle walls. The newly freed man found himself taken to a guestroom in the castle. Within this chamber a servant built a fire to keep him warm. Later, after a heated bath and some time to rest. The stranger was presented with his own clothing. Only the servants had done their best to mend and clean those garments. After he had dressed. A servant came to escort him down to the waiting host.

In this room there was a surprise waiting for the stranger. A feast had been laid out for the two men. While they ate in what was obviously a banquet hall. A nearby fireplace kept the two men comfortable. Once seated the host and his guest relaxed and enjoyed the fine meal. Together they spoke of many things and the hours passed in pleasant conversation. Until finally the meal was over. It was at this moment when the royal youth spoke from his heart.

"I do not know what strange fate has brought you to my door. But for as long as you wish to remain in my kingdom you will be my most honored guest. Though I have the love of my people. I do not have anyone to share my thoughts and concerns with. Having spoken to you at length. I have discovered you are in fact an educated man. Knowing this to be true. I have something I wish to show you."

In short order the prince and his guest were standing by a thick door with an inscription upon its heavy surface. In large silver letters, the word; LIBRARY was spelled out. Pushing his way into this room the prince stepped in then moved to one side. He wanted his guest to fully appreciate what lay revealed within this room.

Feeling drawn into the room before him the traveler came to a sudden halt. In shocked surprise he beheld a room filled floor to ceiling with all manner of books. As his eyes widened in amazement at the treasure laid out before him. The stranger could only gaze in awe. Looking around the interior of this chamber. He could not begin to count the number of volumes this room held. From where he stood, it was easy to see there were all manner of books stored here. Some were heavy hardbound volumes. While on other shelves there were loose-leaf manuscripts. No doubt they contained all manner of mysteries. Continuing to stare at the sight before him. There was no telling what a man who valued knowledge might find here.

Smiling at his astonished guest the prince smiled and spoke in a voice of quiet conviction.

"My parents valued books for what they might reveal. A window to a much larger world filled with wonder. Within this room are many rare and unique manuscripts. It is my wish to share this room with you."

CHAPTER FIVE

In the weeks to follow, the harsh Winter storms raged on while the two men enjoyed a warm fellowship of the mind. Spending many hours discussing matters of intellectual interest or simply reading in silence. While outside the thick stone walls of the castle. The blizzards spent their fury against the castle walls. Time passed until at last the bitterly cold storms began to lessen. Then one day the captain of the royal guard came to see his prince. New reports had come from local hunters. The worst of the storms had passed. And the Mountain Ice Wolves had left the valley. The old soldier also reported that the gap into the valley was now open. With a feeling of relief, the prince thanked his loyal captain and asked him to reward the hunters. He also instructed this older man to express his deep appreciation to his soldiers for their devotion.

While the prince was speaking to his loyal servant. A look of deep sadness touched the face of his guest. An expression the man was quick to hide. In the coming days the prince found himself consumed by his royal duties. With the coming of Spring there was much to do. He must now organize the farmers and townsfolk. There were decisions to be made about what crops to sow. While in the villages, there were repairs to be made. Because the Winter storms had been harsh and there was damage to repair.

For his part the guest now faced a different and unhappy task. One he had known would confront him when Spring did arrive. Now with news of the pass opening. The traveler knew he could not put off his need to act. So, he set to work. His plan was simple but it required him to keep silent. For he could not risk informing his host of what he must do. But in his heart, his actions did not feel honorable. Afterall, the two men had become as close as brothers.

However in the end, the older man had known all along this day would come. For he was bound by a duty he must return to. Obligations he had been unable to shoulder while he was trapped in this valley by blizzards and wolves. But now he must return home to resume those responsibilities. Still, he was heavy with sadness as he gathered those items he would need. All the while he wished he could have shared this burden with his younger friend.

But now with the pass open to him it was time for him to depart for his distant home. Even though he knew he must go, he would always treasure the time he had spent with the younger man. But his duty was clear and there was no turning back now that the time had come. So the next morning found the older man prepared to leave. With the provisions he had gathered he headed for the stable. Where he found the stall holding the horse the prince had given him. Quickly and silently, he saddled the horse. With his supplies tied to his mighty steed he was ready to depart.

There was one final obstacle for him to overcome if his journey were to begin. He had to pass through the front gate where two sentries stood watch. Having prepared himself for what he must do. The traveler rode up to the gate as he had done on previous mornings. Approaching the soldiers on duty, he gave them a warm greeting. His concern grew when they noted the travel satchel on his horse. Seeing this, they might refuse to let him leave.

However these men had grown used to his practice of an early morning ride. And they also knew this man was the guest of their prince. For this reason, they felt no need to hold him. When the older man was through the gate he gave a sigh of relief. With one final wave to the guards, he rode on. Knowing in his heart he might never see this castle or his friend again. But as he galloped away, he knew without a doubt his failure to return would be reported. Then at some point, his departure would be relayed to the prince. But by the time this happened he would be through the pass and well on his way.

It was many hours later when a servant went to deliver the news. His guest had been seen leaving the castle, but had not returned. Upon hearing this, the prince sent out men to search in case his friend had been hurt. When the captain of the guard returned. He informed his prince that the older man had been seen leaving the valley. It was at this point the prince was told of the satchel tied to the horse. After questioning the guards who had been on duty at the gate, on patrol and at the pass. The prince was forced to accept the truth. His friend, for reasons unknown had left the castle, possibly never to return.

Finding no fault in the actions of his loyal sentries, a look of sadness touched the face of the prince. However, he knew he must reassure his men that they had done their duty to him. However, the captain of the guard was quick to speak his mind.

With a voice filled with anger the soldier spoke up.

"My Lord, the actions of your guest are those of a thief! If it is your command, I will summon my soldiers and bring the man back! Afterall, he has taken one of your prized stallions."

It took only a moment for the prince to respond. Shaking his head, he spoke in a clear tone of voice.

"No. There is no reason to bring my friend back. The horse was a gift freely given by me. I gave it in honor of our friendship and he freely accepted it."

There followed a few moments of silence before the young prince once again spoke. "I do not understand why my guest felt compelled to depart in this way. However, I am sure there was a very good reason for him doing so. Though I am sad at his leaving, I count myself truly blessed for the time he spent in my company. For he was, and will always be considered my friend!"

Wanting to make his intention clear to his senior captain. He faced the man and issued a command.

"It is by my command that if my friend should return. He is to be welcomed warmly. For he is my friend!"

So life returned to what most in the valley considered normal. But in the castle, there was a gradual change everyone who served there could feel. The prince, who had been filled with an inner peace during the Winter storms. Was now a different young man. Though he moved among them as usual and offered thanks for their hard work. The people were quick to note how unhappy he had become. It was clear to everyone in the valley the cause of his sadness. He missed his friend. The stranger who had filled a void in their young ruler's life and would be missed.

Still, the prince was bound by his royal duties. Each morning, he would visit the fields to speak to the farmers. Or travel to the different villages to see how the repairs were going. But each evening he would return to the castle for his evening meal. After which he would retire to his study to sit in moody silence. And every day that passed, his melancholy remained. Filling the castle and causing concern for those who served this royal youth.

Knowing the responsibilities he had to his kingdom. The young ruler filled his days with work. Seeing to the needs of his people, training his soldiers, and reviewing reports. But in the evening his thoughts would go to the man who had stayed with him during the harsh Winter. Sharing his wisdom and insight on intellectual topics. Or just the mutual companionship as they read in the library.

With the passing of Spring came Summer. Those who served the needs of the prince grew more troubled. Even with their concern growing. The servants continued to go about their duties. But when they would see the young ruler pass them in the hallways. They could be heard to whisper in a tone of voice filled with sadness. "There goes the Lonely Snow Prince."

Then there came a day much like those that had gone before. When his normal habits found him out inspecting the fields. Looking over the lush growing crops the prince found himself nodding. He felt assured that when it came time for them to harvest. There would be plenty of food to last the coming Winter. It was while the royal youth was at this task, a royal guardsman came riding up. Bringing his horse to a halt he spoke quickly. The soldier informed his prince of an unexpected event. A large group was coming through the pass. The sentry had been informed by one of the captains of this arriving group. That a person of great importance would soon arrive.

It was not long before the sound of drums could be heard drawing closer. Leading this large assembled mass of people was an older man dressed as a soldier. He sat upon a beautiful horse. At a command, the magnificent procession came to a halt. The young prince could see how they were dressed. Each of those up front were wearing the finest clothing the prince had ever seen. As the young royal scanned this large company standing before him. He could only wonder at what had brought this group to his kingdom?

Seeing the soldier at the head of this procession. The young prince could only wonder who the real leader was?

Why had these people come here? Who was their leader and what did he want? The prince knew how small his own kingdom was. He only had a small troop of soldiers at his command. His men were well trained, but they would stand little chance against such a force? Feeling his concern growing. The prince was filled with fear for his people.

Watching intently, the ruler of this tiny kingdom had no way of knowing how this scene would play out. As if in response to his silent question, there came an answer. The man who was obviously a senior officer in this mounted troop shouted a command. Instantly, his well-trained soldiers opened a path in their ranks. Through this gap came a man who had to be the leader of these people. He wore garments fit for a king. The cloth was royal blue and had been embroidered with silver thread. While upon his head he wore a crown. This was a symbol denoting his authority as king.

Then as his parents had taught him to do when meeting royalty. The prince called to his soldiers to honor this visiting king. And with a flourish they saluted as they had been commanded. Upon completing this gesture of respect. The prince bowed his head to the king in front of him. In that moment, the king smiled.

Sitting there on his own horse the prince was puzzled. As there was something vaguely familiar about this king. In the next moment the king issued his own command. In response, his soldiers created another open lane. Looking toward the lane, the prince felt a wave of awe go through him. For this was when he saw a horse and rider coming forward. The horse was the most beautiful white steed he had ever seen. But upon its back was a woman of regal beauty. A sight that took his breath away!

CHAPTER SIX

Riding forward to the head of the column was a woman of poise and dignity. She wore self-assuredness as if it were a cloak around her shoulders. Her garments were of a simple design made for traveling. However, their elegance could not be denied. In every way, she was a true princess. While upon her chest she wore a golden pendant. This symbol, proclaiming her royal station.

For the prince it was impossible to look away. Though he had seen beautiful woman many times in his life. This royal princess possessed an inner serene self-assurance he found breathtaking. Her stunning grace touched him deeply. The next thing he noted, was how her flawless skin glowed. To his fevered mind, it was as if she had been kissed by the sun. But her crowning glory was her hair. Beautiful waves flowing down her back the color of spun gold.

Watching her horse shift from side-to-side with nervous energy. For just a moment the prince grew concerned. But this princess maintained her control with an unmatched self-confidence. Noting these characteristics was more than enough to captivated the prince. But the moment came when he saw her smile at him. This was when the young royal was truly lost. For the curve of her lips seemed to convey a secret only she knew.

After a few more moments of prolonged silence, the princess turned to the king. After bowing slightly to show her deepest respect. She spoke in a clear voice that carried to all who were assembled. In a sweet firm tone she let the meaning of her words convey her thoughts. With a true dept of feeling the princess left no doubt for her listeners.

"Father. After your long absence when we thought you lost to us forever. You returned, filling us with renewed joy. In time you told me of how you had come to meet this young princeling. Secrecy being critical to your mission. You did not reveal your true status. This prince had no way of knowing who you were. He could have cast you out to the waiting jaws of death. Instead, he offered you not only shelter. But an honored place in his home. Even now I find myself moved by the actions of this young man." The princess declared.

Then turning to face the young prince who remained stunned and silent. The princess continued.

"As you have taught me. To offer kindness, compassion and true friendship is rare in this world. Then you told me of his library. But most revealing of all was his devotion to his people. And how much he truly cares for their welfare. But royal sire, it broke my heart to hear of his loneliness."

Pausing as if she were choosing her words with the greatest of care. She turned to face the young prince and announced to those around her.

"Such a man needs a partner to share his duty." The princess stated, then paused to take a breath. As if she were summoning her courage for what she would say next.

"If it should please you, my father. I feel moved to act!"

Turning in her saddle the princess raised her hand to signal a waiting maidservant. With a deft touch, the young maid urged her mount forward. When the young maiden was next to her mistress. She handed the princess a small wooden box. A chest of elegant beauty, inlaid in gold and silver scrollwork. A work of art fashioned by a true master craftsman. Though as beautiful as this chest was. It was the contents of the box that would cause the assembled crowd to gasp! A treasure so revered it had been passed down through countless generations.

Urging her steed forward. The stunning royal princess rode up to the awestruck prince. Then with solemn dignity she presented the ornate box to him. With an earnest look on her face. She allowed a timid smile to touch her lips. Then with the slightest of bows she eased her horse back a few steps. Her intent was clear to all who watched this encounter. She wanted him to inspect the gift she had offered him. As the princess waited, she reached down and caressed her horse while she waited in graceful silence.

Looking down at what lay in his hands. This young prince could only marvel at the amazing craftmanship of the chest. Not really knowing what was expected of him in this situation. He turned his gaze back to the waiting princess. A look of confusion on his face sending a clear message. But she gave no sign of understanding his confusion.In response, he felt trapped as the princess continued to wait. Not knowing what else to do, the young prince opened the chest.

When he did, the contents of the chest were exposed to his amazed eyes. Upon seeing what the box contained, the prince was forced to hold his breath. For even in his remote and isolated little kingdom. He had heard of this rare and priceless object. A gem that now lay before him on a folded blanket of royal velvet. An object he never expected to see with his own eyes. The Royal Amber necklace.

It was a treasure created through the process of time and chance. Because in the distant past, a blossom had become coated in sap. It was the flower known as a Snow Rose. And there would never be another one like it! Because this relic from the distant past no longer grew. The only proof it had ever lived at all, was locked in this jewel. A treasure he now held in his hands. To say the prince was startled was to state the obvious.

Then there was an unexpected sound, no louder than the cooing of a Snow Dove. Thankfully, it was enough to bring the young prince out of his daze. Looking toward where the whisper had come. The prince saw the princess watching him, waiting. Looking around, the royal youth knew a response was expected of him. But he was at a complete loss. What was he supposed to do in this situation?

Seeing the look on the young prince's face. The royal princess took the initiative. With a look of serene dignity on her face, she nudged her horse to move forward. Seconds later she had rejoined the prince. Then with her eyes, she looked at the prince then down at the open box in his hands. In the barest whisper, one only he could hear. She told him of the decision he faced.

"This pendant is an offering of marriage. If you agree and freely accept this symbol of my love. You and I will be wed. But my young prince, look around. Everyone is waiting for you to make your decision known. So, will you be my husband?"

Looking deeply into the eyes of this breathtaking beauty beside him. The prince found himself smiling back at this woman who wished to marry him. Retaining a firm hold on the chest with one hand. The prince reached out to clasp the hand offered by the royal princess. Then the two young people turned to face the nearby king. In an act of respect, the two young lovers bowed their heads with dignified grace! Signaling their intention to marry!

On the day of the formal wedding, it was a joyous occasion. Those who lived in this valley were proud and jubilant. Once the wedding was completed a joyful celebration began. An event that lasted for several days. But all things must end and so it was for the visitors and villagers alike. The visiting guests returned to their own lands. While the villagers went back to their normal lives. Because there was the season of Winter to prepare for.

As for the royal couple, they took up their duties with an intense devotion. Each day one or both rulers of this tiny kingdom would visit with the people. Offering their help, wherever it was needed. Their happy union obvious to all who saw them. With the passing of the years, their names were lost in the mists of time.

But stories never truly die. They come down through the telling of folktales, legends, and fables. Tales to teach, enlighten and encourage us to be kind and compassionate. This story was of friendship and the love it brought to life.

It can show us how caring for others and compassion to a stranger is rewarded. A story you now hold in your hands!

Of a lonely prince in a faraway kingdom who ruled wisely. While demonstrating by his everyday actions his kind and compassionate nature. A man who would come to be known by a far more telling title.

The Snow Prince

The End

Printed in the USA
CPSIA information can be obtained
at www.ICGtesting.com
CBHW060112280924
15036CB00011B/51